1 Introduction

Firms often interact with their rivals in several distinct geographic or product markets. For example, airlines compete in different city-pair markets, pharmaceutical manufacturers compete in treatment markets for different ailments, while conglomerates and multinationals compete across products and national borders. This multimarket contact may reduce the vigor with which such firms compete, as they realize that aggressive behavior in one market may be met by severe reactions in other markets, not only the one in which the disruptive behavior occurred. The possibility of reduced competition associated with multimarket contact creates profit incentives for firms considering either strategic linkage of existing markets or expansion into new markets with the hope of sustaining higher degrees of collusion. In turn, the possibility of these incentives may cause concern to antitrust agencies trying to prevent anticompetitive behavior.

From the perspective of applications, one weakness of existing multimarket contact theory is that it assumes that firms have perfect information about all relevant strategic variables. In practice, this assumption is unlikely to hold, and it is well known that such imperfect information can impede firms' collusive efforts.[1] Given the benefits associated with multimarket contact in perfect information settings, it is important to consider multimarket contact in a way that incorporates uncertainty. To that end, this paper examines the incentive for joint decision making and the potential for anticompetitive harm arising from multimarket contact in markets characterized by imperfect information regarding demand fluctuations. It is conceivable that the possibility of "mistakes" caused by noise in the marketplace may make strategically linking markets an unprofitable course of action. If so, then multimarket contact should be less of a concern to antitrust agencies and should be less of a strategic consideration for firms.

The potential effect of multimarket contact in perfect information settings previously has been explored by economists. In their 1990 paper, Bernheim and Whinston (hereinafter BW) formalized both conventional wisdom and anecdotal evidence regarding the ability of firms engaged in competition across several markets to use that contact to blunt competitive forces. In the context of repeated Bertrand competition with homogenous products, the authors illustrate how firms may use slack enforcement power in one market to sustain collusion in another market that otherwise would be unsustainable. The slack enforcement power mathematically is embodied in the looseness of the incentive constraints that must be satisfied for joint profit maximization, and that power is "used" in another market by pooling the incentive constraints together. For example, it is well

---

[1]For example, see Green and Porter [1984].

1

known that, in an infinitely repeated Bertrand duopoly with homogenous goods and constant marginal costs, the discount factor, δ, must weakly exceed $\frac{1}{2}$ for supracompetitive prices to arise in equilibrium. Similarly, in a market with a per period discount factor of δ^2, δ must weakly exceed $\sqrt{\frac{1}{2}} \approx 0.707$ to sustain supracompetitive prices. If the incentive constraints in the two markets are added together, then the pooled incentive constraint is $\delta + \delta^2 \geq 1$. In this instance, δ need only exceed 0.618 for the constraint to be satisfied. Thus, multimarket contact, as embodied by the pooling of incentive constraints, enlarges the set of discount factors for which collusion in both markets is sustainable.

To illustrate how a stochastic element might reduce the effectiveness of multimarket contact, suppose firms use grim strategies to enforce collusive behavior. That is, each firm responds to a low firm-specific demand realization, whose cause is unknown but is either a negative demand shock or a rival's price cutting, by setting price at the competitive level thereafter. In equilibrium there are no deviations from the collusive price, so price warfare is induced solely by the negative demand shocks.[2] Suppose there are two markets, each of which receives a negative demand shock with probability $\frac{1}{4}$. If the markets are considered in isolation, then the probabilities of being in any particular configuration of collusive and non-collusive phases are shown in the first row of Table 1. If the two markets are strategically linked in a multimarket contact sense, then the strategies employed may be such that collusion breaks down in both markets if there is a negative shock in at least one market. In that instance, the probabilities of being in any particular configuration of collusive and non-collusive phases are shown in the second row of Table 1. As is evident, the middle ground is lost; that is, the multimarket linkage eliminates the possibility of low-grade competition as opposed to either full competition or full collusion.

Table 1

Collusion in Both	Collusion in One	Collusion in None
9/16	6/16	1/16
9/16	0	7/16

Though the candidate strategies in the preceding example obviously are too simple, they do raise the possibility that strategic linkage of markets may not increase profits when firms have imperfect information. Gertner and McCutcheon [1994] (hereinafter GM) is a recent paper that

---

[2]Note that the price wars still must occur, else there will be incentives for firms secretly to cut price.

provides an initial examination of this issue. In addition to a number of interesting applications, the authors demonstrate that the superiority of joint decision making proven in BW can be extended to markets that are identical ex ante but that are subject to unobservable and possibly correlated demand shocks. This conclusion contrasts with the result in BW for identical markets under perfect information, which BW refers to as an "irrelevance result," and it illustrates the role that uncertainty can play in enhancing the effectiveness of joint decision making in multimarket contact settings. As GM's main interest with respect to multimarket contact theory is the preceding point, they restrict their model to a symmetric environment with symmetric treatment of each market. The necessity of symmetry stems from their use of a punishment scheme that differs from the one I employ.

The present paper's model contrasts with GM's model in two primary respects. First, it permits differences in the degree of demand uncertainty across markets, while GM's model assumes the markets are symmetric. This asymmetry leads to richer results regarding the effect of multimarket contact. In particular, I find in several situations that firms have no incentive to strategically link markets, even though naively pooling incentive constraints suggests that multimarket contact is profitable. Second, my model assumes the demand shocks are uncorrelated, while GM's model allows correlation of the demand shocks across markets. Given that GM examines the effect of correlation in the symmetric model, I feel that the computational cost of including correlation in the asymmetric model outweighs the benefits.

My analysis has three primary conclusions. First, linkage of one market with perfect information and another with imperfect information may not increase profits, despite the slack in incentive constraints exploited in perfect information models. Second, multimarket contact does not increase profits if each market has *too little* uncertainty. Third, profits in a market in which some collusion initially can be sustained can increase following linkage with a market in which no collusion initially can be sustained. The central theme of these results is that a market must generate sufficiently noisy signals for it to benefit another market through strategic linkage. This contrasts with the finding in individual markets that collusion decreases as the level of noise increases. This insight is useful to parties involved in antitrust enforcement and litigation. It also is useful to firms considering either strategic linkage of existing markets or expansion into new markets with the hope of sustaining higher degrees of collusion.

The first result holds if any collusion can be sustained in the market with imperfect information, and in some cases if no collusion can be sustained in the market with imperfect information. In the first instance, the result follows from the inability to exploit the excess punishment power that exists in the market with perfect information. Multimarket contact is exploited by decreasing the payoff following negative shocks in both markets, but there never will be such shocks in the market with perfect information. Hence, the threatened lower punishment never will be invoked, and therefore has no deterrent effect on the incentive to deviate in the market with imperfect information. In the second instance, the result follows if the market with imperfect information exhibits too much demand uncertainty. In this case, though firms *could* link the markets while satisfying all necessary constraints, doing so would be less profitable than keeping the markets separate. The frequently occurring shocks in the market with imperfect information have a destabilizing effect on the market with perfect information.

The intuition for the second result is straightforward. The benefit associated with multimarket contact is the coordination of punishments it permits. In equilibrium no firm actually defects from the collusive price, and price wars occur even though it is known that no firm defected. Multimarket contact is exploited by increasing the payoff following bad outcomes in only one market while decreasing the payoff following bad outcomes in both markets. However, if there is too little uncertainty, then there is little chance of even one market having a bad outcome, let alone both. In this instance, a firm's incentive is to defect in one market, rely on the low likelihood that the other market has a low demand realization, and thus avoid the increased punishment. The defecting firm then enjoys the increased payoff following a bad outcome in only one market, relative to the non-coordinated equilibrium, all the while professing its innocence about defection and appealing to bad luck or the law of large numbers to explain the ever increasing string of low demand realizations in one of the markets. While it seems this problem could be eliminated by even more severe punishment when both markets experience a negative demand shock, there is a limit to how strongly one can punish apparent deviations. This limitation on the severity of punishment, coupled with the low likelihood of the punishment being induced, prevents multimarket contact from increasing profits.

In contrast, the third result is that if some collusion initially can be sustained in one market, but not in another, then multimarket contact may increase profits in the initially collusive market. This is orchestrated by increasing the payoff following a bad outcome only in the initially collusive market, while decreasing the payoff following a bad outcome in both markets. Knowing that they will receive a larger payoff even if the outcome in the initially collusive market is bad, it appears that a firm's incentive is to defect in that market. However, the high likelihood that the *other*

4

market will experience a bad demand shock is enough to dissuade the firm from defecting and increasing the likelihood that both markets will have negative outcomes. In this instance, there exist severe enough punishments such that one can increase profits yet prevent deviation in the initially collusive market.

The next section presents an oligopoly supergame in which firms have imperfect information about the level of demand and their rival's actions. Section 3 extends this model to consider multimarket contact between a market with perfect information and one with imperfect information. This simple method shows how the strategic linkage of markets does not necessarily enhance the ability of firms to collude, despite the slack in incentive constraints that was exploited in BW. Section 4 extends the model further, by assuming imperfect information exists in *both* markets. There I find greater support for the initial findings in BW and discuss the difference in predictions of the results in sections 3 and 4. Section 5 briefly concludes.

2 Collusion in the Face of Uncertainty

This section presents a one-market model of a repeated game with uncertainty taken from Chapter 6 of Tirole [1988].[3] Two firms 1 and 2, each with marginal cost c, choose prices every period for a product sold in market A. A firm's price offer is not seen by its rival. The firms' products are perfect substitutes, so consumers always purchase from the low price firm. Assume that demand is split evenly between the two firms in the event of a tie. In each period, there are two possible states of demand. With probability α_A there is no demand in that period, while with probability $1 - \alpha_A$ demand is given by $D(p)$. Denote the unique monopoly price and profit in the "high demand state" by p^m and π^m, respectively. The realizations of demand are assumed to be independently and identically distributed over time. This is a Bertrand version of the model employed in Green and Porter [1984]. Examples of markets with similar informational characteristics include wholesale markets for cement and lumber.

A note on terminology. I refer to an increase in α_A as an increase in uncertainty, in the sense that for a higher α_A and a given strategy for a firm's rival, a firm assigns lower probability to a zero-profit outcome's being the result of a deviation by its rival as opposed to a low demand shock.

In the finitely repeated game, both firms charge c each period. In the supergame, I solve for the

---

[3]I describe the model only briefly. Readers wishing for a fuller treatment should see Section 6.7.1 in Tirole [1988]. As this model is a prelude to those used in succeeding sections, I carefully show how to solve for the highest sustainable payoffs. In the later sections most of the mathematical arguments are relegated to the Appendix.

highest payoff associated with a symmetric sequential equilibrium (SSE).[4,5] This solution follows the method demonstrated by Abreu, Pearce, and Stacchetti [1986,1990] (hereinafter APS). The reason for using such a tool is clear: In order to make convincing statements about the effect of multimarket contact on the ability to collude, it is necessary to find the highest possible payoffs for the firms. This is particularly true regarding claims that multimarket contact does not increase profits.

A brief description of the APS methodology is in order. Of primary importance for the present analysis is the insight that a repeated game, much like a dynamic programming problem, may be decomposed into a family of static games. Consider play following the first period of an SSE. The SSE specifies successor SSEs to be followed in each state of the world after the first period. These successor SSEs have associated payoffs. If the truncated game for each state of the world following the first period is simply replaced by the payoff to the associated successor SSE, then this new game's equilibrium is exactly the first period behavior specified by the original SSE. This approach is analogous to using backward induction to determine the subgame perfect Nash equilibrium in a finite extensive form game. The APS methodology permits one to concentrate on payoffs rather than strategies, which is useful because the strategies potentially are quite complicated.

Let $\mathcal{V} \in \Re$ denote the set of payoffs of all SSEs for the game under consideration. $\mathcal{V}$ is nonempty (setting $p = c$ forever is an SSE) and is compact.[6] Thus, there exists $\overline{V}$, the largest element of $\mathcal{V}$, which is associated with an SSE I denote $\overline{\sigma}$. In the first period of play, $\overline{\sigma}$ specifies that firms set price $\overline{p}$, receiving $\frac{\overline{\pi}}{2}$ with probability $(1 - \alpha_A)$ and receiving 0 with probability α_A. Given the structure of uncertainty, in equilibrium there are only two common knowledge events following the price-setting in period one: Either both firms received a profit or at least one firm did not receive a profit. That is, the finest partition of the information sets on which the firms agree is $\{\{W\},\{X,Y,Z\}\}$ in Table 2. For example, if market demand is high and firm 2 undercuts firm 1, then the firms both could not say that they are in state Y. Firm 1 is unsure whether it received no profit because firm 2 undercut, state Y, or because demand was low, state Z.

---

[4]The restriction to symmetric equilibria is natural given the symmetric nature of the problem. See Abreu, Pearce, and Stacchetti [1990] for a discussion of asymmetric equilibria.

[5]Note that this differs from the treatment in Tirole [1988], which examines an equilibrium consisting of a collusive phase and a punishment phase. In the collusive phase, both firms charge p^m until one firm earns zero profit. Seeing zero profit triggers a punishment phase lasting T_A periods in which both firms charge c. At the end of T_A periods, play reverts to the collusive phase. This method does not guarantee the highest SSE payoff, though it can be shown that it actually *does* generate the highest payoff. The problem with using this method in a multimarket contact setting is discussed in the next section.

[6]$\mathcal{V}$ clearly is bounded, and a limit argument shows that it is closed.

Table 2

	2 received a profit	2 received no profit
1 received a profit	W	X
1 received no profit	Y	Z

Given the two common knowledge events following first period play, $\bar{\sigma}$ specifies two SSEs truncated to the remaining game. Call these truncated SSEs σ^p and σ^c, as mnemonics for punishment and collusion, respectively. These truncated SSEs have associated payoffs V^p and V^c, which both are elements of $\mathcal{V}$. In what follows I am unconcerned with the strategies specified in σ^p and σ^c, just the associated payoffs. The payoff to $\bar{\sigma}$ is

$$\bar{V} = (1 - \alpha_A) \left[\frac{\bar{\pi}}{2} + \delta V^c \right] + \alpha_A \left[\delta V^p \right]. \tag{1}$$

I wish to maximize $\bar{V}$ with respect to $\bar{\pi}$, V^p, and V^c, subject to the following constraints:

$$(1 - \alpha_A) \left[\frac{\bar{\pi}}{2} + \delta V^c \right] + \alpha_A \left[\delta V^p \right] \geq (1 - \alpha_A) \left[\bar{\pi} + \delta V^p \right] + \alpha_A \left[\delta V^p \right] \tag{2}$$

$$0 \leq V^c \leq \bar{V} \tag{3}$$

$$0 \leq V^p \leq \bar{V} \tag{4}$$

$$0 \leq \bar{\pi} \leq \pi^m \tag{5}$$

Equation (2) is an incentive compatibility constraint, according to which the expected profit from colluding must weakly exceed the expected profit from defecting. Equations (3) through (5) are constraints that embody both individual rationality (each firm always can achieve a payoff of 0 by setting $p = c$) and feasibility (e.g. $\bar{\pi}$ must be weakly less than the monopoly profit, π^m). To save space, later in the analysis I simply will refer to equations such as (3) through (5) as feasibility constraints, and usually will not show them in the text.

There are two immediate conclusions from the form of the maximization problem: First, because V^c increases the objective function and relaxes (2) when increased, $V^c = \bar{V}$. Intuitively, if the firms receive their share of the collusive profits in the current period, then they continue with the same behavior in the next period. Second, (2) must bind. If it did not, then one could increase V^p, still satisfy (2), yet increase $\bar{V}$. That is, the firms should not punish poor market outcomes any more than is necessary to prevent deviation, because the demand variability ensures that price wars will

7

occur even though no firm defects.

Using $V^c = \overline{V}$ and the result that (2) holds with equality, I can rewrite the problem to maximize

$$\overline{V} = \frac{(1 - \alpha_A)\frac{\overline{\pi}}{2} + \alpha_A \delta V^p}{1 - (1 - \alpha_A)\delta}. \tag{6}$$

subject to

$$V^p = \frac{[2(1 - \alpha_A)\delta - 1]\overline{\pi}}{2\delta(1 - \delta)} \tag{7}$$

and the remaining feasibility constraints. From (7) it is clear that if $(1 - \alpha_A)\delta < \frac{1}{2}$, then $\overline{\pi} = 0$, $V^p = 0$, and hence $\overline{V} = 0$. This condition nicely generalizes the standard Bertrand result that $\delta \geq \frac{1}{2}$ (with $\alpha_A = 0$) is necessary to sustain supracompetitive pricing.

If $(1 - \alpha_A)\delta \geq \frac{1}{2}$, then substitute δV^p from (7) into (6) to yield

$$\overline{V} = \frac{(1 - 2\alpha_A)\overline{\pi}}{2(1 - \delta)}.$$

The right hand side of this expression is maximized, while still satisfying (7) and the feasibility constraints, at $\overline{\pi} = \pi^m$, so

$$\overline{V} = \frac{(1 - 2\alpha_A)\pi^m}{2(1 - \delta)}.$$

The following proposition summarizes the results.

Proposition 1 *Supracompetitive prices cannot be sustained if either the probability of low demand is too high, or firms care too little about the future, and conversely. Formally, if $(1 - \alpha_A)\delta < \frac{1}{2}$, then $\overline{\pi} = 0$, $V^p = 0$, and hence $\overline{V} = 0$. If $(1 - \alpha_A)\delta \geq \frac{1}{2}$, then*

$$\overline{V} = \frac{(1 - 2\alpha_A)\pi^m}{2(1 - \delta)}.$$

and

$$V^p = \frac{[2(1 - \alpha_A)\delta - 1]\pi^m}{2\delta(1 - \delta)}.$$

Not surprisingly, the maximum payoff is increasing in δ and is decreasing in α_A, the degree of uncertainty. The intuition for the condition $(1 - \alpha_A)\delta \geq \frac{1}{2}$ has to do with the feasibility of punishment.[7] Suppose that $(1 - \alpha_A)\delta < \frac{1}{2}$ and that $V^p = 0$, but that firms attempt to set a price

---

[7]The feasibility of punishment also lies at the heart of the incentive constraint in a market with perfect information, though that interpretation often is overlooked. If one solves the perfect information problem and considers the largest

greater than marginal cost. From (2), it must be the case that $\delta V^c \geq \frac{\overline{\pi}}{2}$. If δ is too low, then a firm cares too little about the future to be deterred from cheating on the tacit agreement. The gain from cheating earned today, $\frac{\overline{\pi}}{2}$, outweighs the loss from cheating incurred tomorrow, δV^c. If α_A is too high, then a firm expects future collusive profits to be low. That is, as α_A increases, $\overline{V}$ increasingly is determined by V^p, which equals 0. Therefore, the loss from cheating incurred tomorrow, δV^c, is outweighed by the gain from cheating earned today, $\frac{\overline{\pi}}{2}$. Thus, even though a firm knows that if it defects it will get a payoff of zero for the rest of the game, the punishment already is so likely to be induced following tomorrow's play that today the firm is willing to induce punishment for sure and take the chance of getting an increased payoff in the current period.

3 Multimarket Contact With Partial Uncertainty

The previous section illustrates how imperfect information about demand can impede firms' collusive efforts. Having learned from the BW analysis that multimarket contact increases profitability, a firm might consider linking a market that has imperfect information with a market that has perfect information. For example, price and quantity information could be easy to monitor, while advertising or R&D outlays could be very difficult to monitor. Firms might see a strategic linkage of prices and advertising expenditures as their best opportunity to increase profits, as opposed to a linkage of two markets that both have imperfect information. I show that in some instances this intuition is incorrect.

Suppose firms 1 and 2 now compete in two markets, A and B, and choose prices in each market in each period. A firm's prices are not seen by its rival. For simplicity, marginal cost is c in each market and for each firm. With probability α_A, market A is in the "low demand state," facing no demand for the product. With probability $1 - \alpha_A$, market A is in the "high demand state" with demand $D(p)$. Market B has no demand fluctuations, with firms always facing demand $D(p)$.[8] Assume that the realizations of demand in market A are independently and identically distributed across time. If the firms treat the markets separately, then the maximum profits for the firms in this non-coordinated equilibrium are those found in Section 2.

This model adds a small amount of uncertainty to offer an extremely simple way to study the interaction between imperfect information and multimarket contact. In fact, by having uncertainty in only one market, the analysis looks much like that in Section 2. Denote by $\mathcal{V}_J$ the non-empty and

---

payoff following defection consistent with maximal collusion, then it becomes clear that the maximal payoff following defection approaches zero as $\delta \downarrow \frac{1}{2}$.

[8]The assumption that the markets are identical except that one is more likely to have low demand than is the other serves to highlight the effect that uncertainty has on the decision to link markets strategically.

compact set of SSE payoffs for this game permitting decisionmaking jointly across markets. Let $\overline{\sigma}_J$ be the SSE which yields the largest element of $\mathcal{V}_J$, $\overline{V}_J$. In the first period of play, $\overline{\sigma}_J$ specifies that firms set prices $\overline{p}_A$ and $\overline{p}_B$, receiving payoff $\frac{\overline{\pi}_B}{2}$ with probability one and payoff $\frac{\overline{\pi}_A}{2}$ with probability $(1 - \alpha_A)$. As in Section 2, in equilibrium there are only two common knowledge events following the price-setting in period one: Either both firms received a profit in market A, or at least one firm did not.[9] $\overline{\sigma}_J$ specifies two SSEs truncated to the remaining game, one for each common knowledge contingency. Call these σ_A^p and σ^c, with associated payoffs V_A^p and V^c, both elements of $\mathcal{V}_J$. Other relevant SSEs, which come into play only out of equilibrium, are σ_B^p and σ_{AB}^p, which are the SSEs specified by $\overline{\sigma}_J$ following a defection in B or in both A and B. These SSEs have associated payoffs V_B^p and V_{AB}^p. The payoff to $\overline{\sigma}_J$ is

$$\overline{V}_J = (1 - \alpha_A) \left[\frac{\overline{\pi}_A + \overline{\pi}_B}{2} + \delta V^c \right] + \alpha_A \left[\frac{\overline{\pi}_B}{2} + \delta V_A^p \right]. \tag{8}$$

I wish to maximize $\overline{V}_J$ with respect to $\overline{\pi}_A$, $\overline{\pi}_B$, V_A^p, V_B^p, V_{AB}^p, and V^c, subject to the incentive compatibility constraints below and the feasibility constraints.

$$(1 - \alpha_A) \left[\frac{\overline{\pi}_A + \overline{\pi}_B}{2} + \delta V^c \right] + \alpha_A \left[\frac{\overline{\pi}_B}{2} + \delta V_A^p \right] \geq (1 - \alpha_A) \left[\overline{\pi}_A + \frac{\overline{\pi}_B}{2} + \delta V_A^p \right] + \alpha_A \left[\frac{\overline{\pi}_B}{2} + \delta V_A^p \right] \tag{9}$$

$$(1 - \alpha_A) \left[\frac{\overline{\pi}_A + \overline{\pi}_B}{2} + \delta V^c \right] + \alpha_A \left[\frac{\overline{\pi}_B}{2} + \delta V_A^p \right] \geq (1 - \alpha_A) \left[\frac{\overline{\pi}_A}{2} + \overline{\pi}_B + \delta V_B^p \right] + \alpha_A \left[\overline{\pi}_B + \delta V_{AB}^p \right] \tag{10}$$

$$(1 - \alpha_A) \left[\frac{\overline{\pi}_A + \overline{\pi}_B}{2} + \delta V^c \right] + \alpha_A \left[\frac{\overline{\pi}_B}{2} + \delta V_A^p \right] \geq (1 - \alpha_A) \left[\overline{\pi}_A + \overline{\pi}_B + \delta V_{AB}^p \right] + \alpha_A \left[\overline{\pi}_B + \delta V_{AB}^p \right] \tag{11}$$

The incentive constraints (9)-(11) specify that it must not be profitable for a firm to deviate in market A only, market B only, or both markets A and B, respectively.

As in the single market model, $V^c = \overline{V}_J$; successful collusion is followed by again setting the collusive prices in each market. Also, certainty regarding demand in market B allows strong punishment without fear of mistakenly invoking punishment. Because V_B^p and V_{AB}^p do not affect the objective function and relax the incentive constraints when decreased, any deviation in market

---

[9]At this point, one sees the utility of using the APS methodology versus that used in Tirole [1988] and GM. Specifically, it is not clear how one would specify the punishments with the alternative approach. It is not obvious whether only one length of punishment is used in both markets simultaneously, or whether each market has its own punishment length. Using the latter method, one must specify how the punishment regimes interact. For example, suppose market A is in the punishment regime, while market B has finished punishment and has returned to the collusive equilibrium for that market. Does the market A punishment begin again if there is a defection in B? Using the APS methodology, one ignores the specifics of the punishment profiles and concentrates simply on the payoffs.

B is followed by setting $p = c$ in both markets forever. Therefore, $V_B^p = V_{AB}^p = 0$.

There are three possibilities when the two markets are considered in isolation: collusion may be sustainable in zero, one, or both markets. I consider each possibility separately.

Proposition 2 *If collusion is not sustainable in either market in the non-coordinated equilibrium, then multimarket contact does not increase profits. Formally, if $\delta < \frac{1}{2}$, then $\overline{V}_J = 0$.*

This result is not too surprising, given the result from a standard Bertrand supergame. In this case, neither market has excess enforcement power that can be used to increase collusion in the other market.

Proposition 3 *If collusion is sustainable in both markets in the non-coordinated equilibrium, then multimarket contact does not increase profits. Formally, if $(1 - \alpha_A)\delta \geq \frac{1}{2}$, then*

$$\overline{V}_J = \frac{(1 - 2\alpha_A)\pi^m}{2(1 - \delta)} + \frac{\pi^m}{2(1 - \delta)}.$$

The previous two results appear to be similar to the "irrelevance result" in BW that shows that identical markets do not benefit from multimarket contact. The basic intuition of their irrelevance result is that in isolation either each market already can sustain full collusion (as in Proposition 3), in which case there does not exist a need for multimarket contact, or neither market can sustain any collusion (as in Proposition 2), in which case neither market has excess punishment power to use to increase profits. Though in the present case markets A and B are not identical, under the conditions of Proposition 3 some collusion is possible in both in the non-coordinated equilibrium. What is surprising is that, in isolation, the certain market, with its slack incentive constraint, has excess punishment power,[10] while the uncertain market's incentive constraint is binding and full collusion cannot be sustained. Multimarket contact raises profits by coordinating punishments, in that if a firm cheats in A, then the payoff in B also is lowered. By pooling the incentive constraints it seemingly should be possible to increase the overall level of profits. The flaw in this reasoning is that the probability of entering the punishment phase associated with defection in market A is unchanged following the multimarket link. The payoff following an apparent defection in A cannot be increased with a concomitant decrease in the payoff following low demand realizations in both A and B, as this will induce players to defect in A only in every period. The more severe punishment

---

[10] "Excess punishment power" in a world of perfect information formally means that the payoff following defection does not have to be zero.

never will be invoked, because market B always has high demand. Reducing the payoff following an apparent defection in A, say by switching to less profitable behavior in market B, does not reduce defection in market A, as there already was no defection in equilibrium. Reducing that payoff merely reduces the overall payoff, because the punishment phase is entered only when there is a negative demand shock. If firms already are not cheating, and only enter punishment phases to ensure that they do not cheat, then B's excess power has no place to be applied.

Proposition 3's result suggests that markets in which collusion is possible in isolation do not benefit from multimarket contact, but this is at odds with GM's Proposition 1 that shows that in markets with symmetric uncertainty (and no demand shock correlation) there always are gains to multimarket contact. It seems unlikely that making one market's chance of high demand much more certain reduces the effectiveness of multimarket contact. However, as described in the preceding paragraph, the problem when market B always has high demand is that it is impossible to reduce the payoff following defection in both markets in a way that permits increasing the payoff following a low demand realization in the uncertain market. This reasoning suggests that the problem lies with the certainty associated with market B, and therefore suggests that multimarket contact increases profits even with the smallest degree of uncertainty in market B. I show in the next section, however, that this argument is incorrect.

Proposition 4 *If, in the non-coordinated equilibrium, collusion is sustainable in the certain market but not in the uncertain market, then multimarket contact may increase profits. If uncertainty is the primary hindrance to collusion, then profits do not increase. Formally, suppose $\delta \geq \frac{1}{2}$ and $(1 - \alpha_A)\delta < \frac{1}{2}$. If $\alpha_A \leq \frac{1}{2}$, then*

$$\overline{V}_J = \frac{(1 - 2\alpha_A)\overline{\pi}_A}{2(1 - \delta)} + \frac{\pi^m}{2(1 - \delta)}$$

and

$$V_A^P = \frac{\pi^m}{2(1 - \delta)} - \frac{[1 - 2(1 - \alpha_A)\delta]\,\overline{\pi}_A}{2\delta(1 - \delta)},$$

where

$$\overline{\pi}_A = \min\left[\frac{(2\delta - 1)\pi^m}{1 - 2(1 - \alpha_A)\delta}, \pi^m\right].$$

However, if $\alpha_A > \frac{1}{2}$, then $\overline{p}_A = c$, $\overline{\pi}_A = 0$, and

$$\overline{V}_J = \frac{\pi^m}{2(1 - \delta)}.$$

Multimarket contact is exploited in this instance by decreasing the payoff in market B if there is a bad outcome in market A. This is evident by noting that V_A^p is less than its value in the non-coordinated equilibrium. In that equilibrium, $V_A^p = \frac{\pi^m}{2(1-\delta)}$, which is the payoff associated with perpetual collusion in market B. This optimal strategy for exploiting multimarket contact is effective if there is not too much uncertainty. However, as α_A increases beyond $\frac{1}{2}$, then the increased uncertainty lowers profits if firms insist on strictly linking the two markets. For example, suppose that the pooled incentive constraint, $\delta + (1-\alpha_A)\delta \geq 1$, from the two incentive constraints in the non-coordinated equilibrium, is satisfied. In this instance, Proposition 4 indicates that $\overline{\pi}_A = \pi^m$. If α_A increases beyond $\frac{1}{2}$, then firms still can prevent defection in market A by threatening lower profits in market B, but it is not worth doing so. The amount firms gain by setting $\overline{p}_A > c$ in market A cannot compensate for the loss so frequently incurred in market B. In this instance, the destabilizing nature of the shocks in market A so adversely affects market B that linking the two markets is unprofitable.

Figure 1 illustrates the parameter dependent results of Propositions 2 through 4. In region ABC, to the northeast of $(1-\alpha_A)\delta = \frac{1}{2}$, collusion is sustainable in the two markets without coordination. In that case, multimarket contact does not increase industry profits. In region ACD, in the non-coordinated equilibrium collusion is sustainable in the certain market but is not sustainable in the uncertain market, yet the multimarket contact allows the firms to set the monopoly price in that market. This accords with the intuition from BW, as the line ADF is the locus above which the pooled incentive constraint $(1-\alpha_A)\delta + \delta \geq 1$ is satisfied. Given the previous result, behavior in the following two regions is of interest. First, though the pooled incentive constraint is satisfied in region CDF while the single incentive constraint for the uncertain market is not, multimarket contact does not increase industry profits. The occurs because of the previously described destabilizing nature of the shocks in market A. Thus, simple application of the notion of pooling incentive constraints leads one to overstate the degree to which additional collusion may be sustained using multimarket contact. Second, in the region ADE, though it is *below* the pooled incentive constraint embodied by AD, multimarket contact does permit higher industry profits. These last two observations suggest that the degree of uncertainty plays a larger role in sustaining additional collusion via multimarket contact than does the degree of firms' impatience.[11]

---

[11]One way to examine this more rigorously is to suppose that the two markets have different discount factors. However, this assumption is difficult to justify if the discount factor simply embodies a firm's rate of time preference. If the markets meet with different frequencies or grow at different rates, or if the discount factor also includes some

4 Multimarket Contact With Uncertainty

This section extends the analysis of Section 3 by allowing both markets to be subject to demand uncertainty, which arguably is the most realistic case to consider. Assume the model is identical to the one presented in Section 3, except now market B has low demand with probability α_B, where $0 < \alpha_B \leq \alpha_A$. Furthermore, assume that the realizations of demand are independent across markets and across time. If the firms treat the markets in isolation, then the maximum profits for the firms in the non-coordinated equilibrium are those found in Section 2.

Recalling the notation in Section 3, the firms maximize

$$\overline{V}_J = (1-\alpha_A)(1-\alpha_B)\left[\frac{\overline{\pi}_A + \overline{\pi}_B}{2} + \delta V^c\right] + (1-\alpha_A)\alpha_B\left[\frac{\overline{\pi}_A}{2} + \delta V_B^p\right] + \qquad (12)$$
$$\alpha_A(1-\alpha_B)\left[\frac{\overline{\pi}_B}{2} + \delta V_A^p\right] + \alpha_A\alpha_B\left[\delta V_{AB}^p\right]$$

subject to

$$(1-\alpha_B)\delta\left[V^c - V_A^p\right] + \alpha_B\delta\left[V_B^p - V_{AB}^p\right] \geq \frac{\overline{\pi}_A}{2} \qquad (13)$$

$$(1-\alpha_A)\delta\left[V^c - V_B^p\right] + \alpha_A\delta\left[V_A^p - V_{AB}^p\right] \geq \frac{\overline{\pi}_B}{2} \qquad (14)$$

and

$$(1-\alpha_A)(1-\alpha_B)\delta[V^c - V_{AB}^p] + (1-\alpha_A)\alpha_B\delta[V_B^p - V_{AB}^p] + \alpha_A(1-\alpha_B)\delta[V_A^p - V_{AB}^p] \quad (15)$$
$$\geq \quad (1-\alpha_A)\frac{\overline{\pi}_A}{2} + (1-\alpha_B)\frac{\overline{\pi}_B}{2}$$

I wish to maximize $\overline{V}_J$ with respect to $\overline{\pi}_A$, $\overline{\pi}_B$, V_A^p, V_B^p, V_{AB}^p, and V^c, subject to the incentive compatibility constraints (13)-(15) and the feasibility constraints. As in the single market model, $V^c = \overline{V}_J$; successful collusion is followed by again setting the collusive prices in each market. Multimarket contact is exploited by raising V_A^p, say, while simultaneously decreasing V_B^p or V_{AB}^p to keep the incentive constraints satisfied.

One difference between this approach with imperfect information and BW's approach with perfect information is that with the latter approach one need only be concerned with defection in both markets simultaneously. Given that any deviation can be observed perfectly and dealt with

---

probability that the market permanently collapses, then it is more plausible to assume discount factors differ across markets. In any event, this change in structure, while not qualitatively changing the method of examination, may greatly complicate the analytics.

simply by setting $p = c$ forever, all the V_i^p terms are set to zero, in which case (15) implies both (13) and (14). With imperfect information, one must account for firms' incentives to defect only in one market at a time, and so the incentive constraints in the original problem cannot simply be added together when considering the use of multimarket contact to enhance coordination.

As the first step in the solution process, it can be shown (see Lemma 1 in the Appendix) that the incentive constraints preventing cheating in A or B separately, (13) and (14), both cannot be slack. If both were slack, then it would be the case that $V_A^p = V_B^p = V^c$. If so, then with no reversion to punishment in the event only one market had a bad outcome, the sum of the expected loss from defecting in A only and B only is less than the expected loss from defecting in A and B simultaneously. This is the case because there exists an additional source of loss when defecting in both markets at one time: with such a defection, a firm can go from a good outcome in both markets to a bad outcome in both markets. Such an outcome, *induced by cheating*, cannot occur when defecting in only one market. However, the sum of the expected gains from defecting in A only and B only is identical to the expected gain from defecting in both markets simultaneously, because the demand shocks in the two markets are independent. Consequently, if (13) and (14) both are slack, then (15) must also be slack. However, with demand uncertainty, all three constraints cannot be slack at the joint profit maximizing level.

The finding that at least one of (13) and (14) must bind permits characterization of four situations in which using multimarket contact affects profits. Given the complex interaction between the degree of impatience, δ, and the degrees of uncertainty, α_A and α_B, a complete characterization does not necessarily generate especially useful insights. However, such a characterization can be obtained using results presented in the Appendix.

Proposition 5 *Suppose some collusion can be sustained in each market in the non-coordinated equilibrium. If there is a sufficiently small degree of uncertainty in both markets, then multimarket contact does not increase profits.*

This result is consistent with Proposition 3, in which market B always has high demand, the smallest degree of uncertainty. The intuition for this surprising result is as follows. Recall that multimarket contact is exploited by making incentive compatible punishing less harshly when one bad outcome is observed by punishing more harshly when two bad outcomes are observed. There are limits to how much one can punish deviations, however, and the problem that occurs when α_A and α_B get too small is that it becomes very unlikely that even one market will experience low demand. Hence, a firm's defection strategy will be to defect in one market, be fairly certain that the other market still will have high demand, and thus avoid the harsh punishment while professing its innocence. Such a deviation would be profitable, because the punishment necessary to prevent the deviation entails a negative stream of payoffs in the continuation equilibrium, which violates individual rationality. Thus, the limitation on the severity of punishment, coupled with the low likelihood of the punishment being induced, prevents multimarket contact from increasing profits.

Proposition 6 *Suppose that collusion cannot be sustained in either market in the non-coordinated equilibrium. If each market has a sufficiently high degree of uncertainty, then multimarket contact does not increase profits.*

This result is not too surprising. Even though, due to the other market's high likelihood of having a negative demand shock, cheating in one market is quite likely to induce severe punishment, the low value of future payoffs makes cheating today profitable. Therefore, supracompetitive profits cannot be sustained.

Proposition 7 *Suppose that collusion cannot be sustained in at least one of the markets in the non-coordinated equilibrium. If that market has a sufficiently large degree of uncertainty and the other market has a sufficiently small degree of uncertainty, then multimarket contact increases profits.*

This result is consistent with Proposition 6. The market with a very small degree of uncertainty cannot help increase profits in the market with a large degree of uncertainty, because the probability of having a bad outcome in the more certain market is so low. However, the reverse is true. If a firm cheats in the more certain market, then it is quite likely the less certain market will have a negative shock, thus inducing the severe punishment. Therefore, a firm will not cheat in the more certain market. This permits a much higher payoff following a negative demand shock in market B, as the following example illustrates.

Suppose that $\alpha_A = 0.4$, $\alpha_B = 0.1$, and $\delta = 0.75$. Using the solution obtained in the non-coordinated equilibria, the payoffs are

$$\overline{V}_J = 1.6\pi^m \quad V_A^p = 1.6\pi^m \quad V_B^p = 0.933\pi^m \quad V_{AB}^P = 0.933\pi^m$$

Using Case 3 of Lemma 4 in the Appendix, one can determine that the maximal profits and the

16

associated punishment payoffs when using multimarket contact are

$$\overline{V}_J = 2.2\pi^m \quad V_A^p = 1.8\pi^m \quad V_B^p = 2.2\pi^m \quad V_{AB}^p = 0.033\pi^m$$

By successfully using multimarket contact, the payoff following defection in only market B increases by 136%, in only market A increases by 13%, and in both markets A and B decreases by 96%. Surprisingly, by linking a low noise market with a high noise market, the largest payoff gain is in the low noise market. Note that if α_A decreases to 0.2, then multimarket contact no longer increases profits. Of course, total profits in that case are

$$\overline{V}_J = 2.8\pi^m \quad V_A^p = 2.133\pi^m \quad V_B^p = 2.133\pi^m \quad V_{AB}^p = 1.466\pi^m$$

and they exceed the profits from using multimarket contact with the higher degree of uncertainty in market A. That is, the ability to profitably employ multimarket contact does not make more uncertainty preferable to less.

Proposition 8 *If each market has a moderate degree of uncertainty, then multimarket contact increases profits. This can be true whether or not some collusion initially was sustainable in either market in the non-coordinated equilibrium.*

This result links the preceding three. A market can gain from linkage with another only if it does not have too much or too little uncertainty. Consequently, medium ranges of uncertainty in each market are more conducive to gaining from multimarket contact than from having too much or too little.

The preceding four propositions illustrate how the imperfect information setting relates to the perfect information setting examined by BW. In BW, the authors present an "irrelevance result," in which they give conditions under which multimarket contact does not increase profits. The basic reasoning is that in the non-coordinated equilibrium, either collusion can be sustained in both markets, or collusion cannot be sustained in either market. Thus, there is no benefit to linking the markets. Propositions 5, 6, and 8 offer continuity between the all-or-nothing outcomes in the non-coordinated equilibrium of the perfect information setting. If $\alpha_A = \alpha_B = 0$, then full collusion can be sustained in the non-coordinated equilibrium, and multimarket contact does not increase profits. Multimarket contact does not increase profits until α_A and α_B increase to moderate levels, including levels such that no collusion is sustainable in the non-coordinated equilibrium. Finally, as α_A and α_B increase even further, beyond the point at which no collusion can be sustained in the non-coordinated equilibrium, multimarket contact does not increase profits.

5 Conclusion

This paper examines the effect on tacit collusion of the interaction between imperfect information and multimarket contact. When firms have imperfect information about the state of demand, I show that reliance on multimarket contact theory confined to markets with perfect information leads one to misstate the effect of multimarket contact on the degree of sustainable collusion. This misstatement is not simply a question of the magnitude of increased profits, but is a question of the existence of profit increases. The central theme of the results is that a market must generate sufficiently noisy signals for it to benefit another market through strategic linkage. This outcome is surprising, given one's intuition that linking a high noise market to a low noise market might lead to shocks from the high noise market spreading to and adversely affecting the low noise one. Such destabilization does occur, but not in all instances in which it seems plausible. This insight is useful to parties involved in antitrust enforcement and litigation. It also is useful to firms considering either strategic linkage of existing markets or expansion into new markets with the hope of sustaining higher degrees of collusion.

I introduce imperfect information into the multimarket contact framework in two stages. First, I examine the strategic linkage of two markets, one that is subject to demand uncertainty and one that is not. A firm presumably would consider such a link more valuable than a linkage of two markets that both are subject to unseen demand fluctuations. However, such a link may not increase profits, despite the slack in incentive constraints exploited in perfect information models. The results indicate that the benefits from multimarket contact do not arise simply from the presence of excess punishment power, but also from the existence of an outlet through which any excess punishment power can be applied. Second, I examine the arguably more realistic setting in which demand uncertainty is present in and asymmetric across both markets. If both markets have too little uncertainty, then multimarket contact does not increase profits. The reason for this is that it becomes impossible to punish defection in both markets severely enough to make defection in only one market undesirable. If firms attempt to secure additional industry profits, then an individual firm's incentive is to cheat in one market, bank on the low likelihood of the other market having a demand shock that will trigger severe punishment, then simply appeal to bad luck or the law of large numbers while professing its innocence. While it seems this problem could be eliminated by even more severe punishment when both markets experience a negative demand

18

shock, there is a limit to how strongly one can punish apparent deviations. For moderate levels of uncertainty in each market, multimarket contact increases profits. Finally, I show that a market with a great deal of uncertainty, in which collusion cannot be sustained in isolation, sometimes can be used to bolster collusion in a market subject to more stable demand.

These results are convincing in light of earlier work for two reasons. First, I use a simple extension of the perfect information model employed by Bernheim and Whinston [1990], so their work provides a good benchmark for comparison. Second, I solve for the highest sustainable payoffs for the firms, so the results showing that multimarket contact has no role do not rely on my inability to find a suitably profitable collusive scheme. In this setting, the solution concept I employ from Abreu, Pearce, and Stacchetti [1986, 1990] is both powerful and simple.

The model offers testable predictions that likely can be evaluated within the experimental literature examining the effect of multimarket contact on firms' prices and profits.[12] Because it is difficult to quantify the degree of uncertainty in actual markets, it is likely that experiments designed to measure demand uncertainty's impact on the effectiveness of multimarket contact as a tool for increasing profits will be more useful than trying to discern the effects in field data.[13]

There are at least four ways one may consider extending the theoretical analysis. First, one may increase the number of firms or markets. Second, one may permit different numbers of firms in the different markets, as is done in Section 4 of Bernheim and Whinston [1990]. These two extensions should have no qualitative effect on the results. Third, one may add correlation of demand shocks across markets, as is done in Gertner and McCutcheon [1994]. Their analysis shows that correlation affects the nature of the results in the symmetric model. Fourth, one could consider a homogenous product Cournot model or a differentiated product Bertrand model to check the sensitivity of the results to the discontinuous nature of the profit function used in this paper's model.

Appendix

Analyzing Section 3

I wish to maximize $\overline{V}_J$ with respect to $\overline{\pi}_A$, $\overline{\pi}_B$, V_A^p, V_B^p, V_{AB}^p, and V^c, subject to the feasibility constraints and the following incentive constraints:

$$(1-\alpha_A)\left[\frac{\overline{\pi}_A+\overline{\pi}_B}{2}+\delta V^c\right]+\alpha_A\left[\frac{\overline{\pi}_B}{2}+\delta V_A^p\right] \geq (1-\alpha_A)\left[\overline{\pi}_A+\frac{\overline{\pi}_B}{2}+\delta V_A^p\right]+\alpha_A\left[\frac{\overline{\pi}_B}{2}+\delta V_A^p\right] \quad (16)$$

---

[12]See Feinberg and Sherman [1985, 1988] and Phillips and Mason [1992].

[13]See Evans and Kessides [1994], Barla [1994], and Singal [1996] (airlines); Jans and Rosenbaum [1997], Parker and Roller [1994] (cement and cellular phones).

19

$$(1-\alpha_A)\left[\frac{\overline{\pi}_A+\overline{\pi}_B}{2}+\delta V^c\right]+\alpha_A\left[\frac{\overline{\pi}_B}{2}+\delta V^p_A\right] \geq (1-\alpha_A)\left[\frac{\overline{\pi}_A}{2}+\overline{\pi}_B+\delta V^p_B\right]+\alpha_A\left[\overline{\pi}_B+\delta V^p_{AB}\right] \quad (17)$$

$$(1-\alpha_A)\left[\frac{\overline{\pi}_A+\overline{\pi}_B}{2}+\delta V^c\right]+\alpha_A\left[\frac{\overline{\pi}_B}{2}+\delta V^p_A\right] \geq (1-\alpha_A)\left[\overline{\pi}_A+\overline{\pi}_B+\delta V^p_{AB}\right]+\alpha_A\left[\overline{\pi}_B+\delta V^p_{AB}\right] \quad (18)$$

(16) through (18) force equilibrium payoffs to exceed those from defecting in A only, B only, or A and B together, respectively. They may be simplified to obtain

$$\delta\left[V^c-V^p_A\right] \geq \frac{\overline{\pi}_A}{2} \quad (19)$$

$$(1-\alpha_A)\delta\left[V^c-V^p_B\right]+\alpha_A\delta\left[V^p_A-V^p_{AB}\right] \geq \frac{\overline{\pi}_B}{2} \quad (20)$$

$$(1-\alpha_A)\delta\left[V^c-V^p_{AB}\right]+\alpha_A\delta\left[V^p_A-V^p_{AB}\right] \geq (1-\alpha_A)\frac{\overline{\pi}_A}{2}+\frac{\overline{\pi}_B}{2} \quad (21)$$

Because V^p_B and V^p_{AB} do not enter the objective function, they create the most slack in the incentive constraints by being as small as possible. Thus, $V^p_B = V^p_{AB} = 0$, so that any defection in B is followed by setting $p = c$ in both markets forever. Given the preceding condition, (20) holds whenever (21) holds, so (20) is superfluous, and the constraints are

$$\delta\left[V^c-V^p_A\right] \geq \frac{\overline{\pi}_A}{2} \quad (22)$$

$$(1-\alpha_A)\delta V^c+\alpha_A\delta V^p_A \geq (1-\alpha_A)\frac{\overline{\pi}_A}{2}+\frac{\overline{\pi}_B}{2} \quad (23)$$

If $\alpha_A = 0$, then this collapses to the perfect information problem. If $\alpha_A > 0$, then (22) binds. If it did not, then one could increase V^p_A, increasing $\overline{V}_J$ without violating the two constraints. Using (22) in (23) and the objective function yields

$$\overline{V}_J = (1-2\alpha_A)\frac{\overline{\pi}_A}{2}+\delta V^c+\frac{\overline{\pi}_B}{2} \quad (24)$$

and

$$\delta V^c \geq \frac{\overline{\pi}_A}{2}+\frac{\overline{\pi}_B}{2}. \quad (25)$$

Now $V^c = \overline{V}_J$, so

$$\overline{V}_J = \left(\frac{1}{1-\delta}\right)\left[(1-2\alpha_A)\frac{\overline{\pi}_A}{2}+\frac{\overline{\pi}_B}{2}\right] \quad (26)$$

and

$$[2(1-\alpha_A)\delta-1]\frac{\overline{\pi}_A}{2}+(2\delta-1)\frac{\overline{\pi}_B}{2} \geq 0. \quad (27)$$

20

Proof of Proposition 2: If $\delta < \frac{1}{2}$, then (27) is satisfied only if $\bar{\pi}_A = \bar{\pi}_B = 0$. This implies $\overline{V}_J = 0.$ □

Proof of Proposition 3: If $(1 - \alpha_A)\delta \geq \frac{1}{2}$, then $\delta \geq \frac{1}{2}$ and both $\bar{\pi}_A$ and $\bar{\pi}_B$ can be as large as possible and still satisfy (27). As $\bar{\pi}_A$ and $\bar{\pi}_B$ enter the objective function positively, taking $\bar{\pi}_A = \pi^m$ and $\bar{\pi}_B = \pi^m$ yields the maximum payoff. □

Proof of Proposition 4: If $\delta \geq \frac{1}{2}$ and $(1 - \alpha_A)\delta < \frac{1}{2}$, then letting $\bar{\pi}_B = \pi^m$ increases the objective function and relaxes (27) by as much as possible. However, $(1 - \alpha_A)\delta < \frac{1}{2}$ implies that the $\frac{\bar{\pi}_A}{2}$ term in (27) enters negatively. If $\alpha_A > \frac{1}{2}$, then $\frac{\bar{\pi}_A}{2}$ also enters the objective function negatively. Therefore, $\overline{V}_J$ is maximized by letting $\bar{\pi}_A = 0$. If $\alpha_A \leq \frac{1}{2}$, then $\frac{\bar{\pi}_A}{2}$ enters the objective function positively. Therefore, $\overline{V}_J$ is maximized by letting $\bar{\pi}_A$ be as large as possible, subject to (27). This occurs when

$$\bar{\pi}_A = \min\left[\frac{(2\delta - 1)\pi^m}{1 - 2(1 - \alpha_A)\delta}, \pi^m\right]. \tag{28}$$

Analyzing Section 4

I wish to maximize $\overline{V}_J$ with respect to $\bar{\pi}_A$, $\bar{\pi}_B$, V_A^p, V_B^p, V_{AB}^p, and V^c, subject to the feasibility constraints and the following incentive constraints:

$$(1 - \alpha_A)(1 - \alpha_B)\left[\frac{\bar{\pi}_A + \bar{\pi}_B}{2} + \delta V^c\right] + (1 - \alpha_A)\alpha_B\left[\frac{\bar{\pi}_A}{2} + \delta V_B^p\right] \tag{29}$$

$$+ \alpha_A(1 - \alpha_B)\left[\frac{\bar{\pi}_B}{2} + \delta V_A^p\right] + \alpha_A\alpha_B\left[\delta V_{AB}^p\right]$$

$$\geq (1 - \alpha_A)(1 - \alpha_B)\left[\bar{\pi}_A + \frac{\bar{\pi}_B}{2} + \delta V_A^p\right] + (1 - \alpha_A)\alpha_B\left[\bar{\pi}_A + \delta V_{AB}^p\right]$$

$$+ \alpha_A(1 - \alpha_B)\left[\frac{\bar{\pi}_B}{2} + \delta V_A^p\right] + \alpha_A\alpha_B\left[\delta V_{AB}^p\right]$$

and

$$(1 - \alpha_A)(1 - \alpha_B)\left[\frac{\bar{\pi}_A + \bar{\pi}_B}{2} + \delta V^c\right] + (1 - \alpha_A)\alpha_B\left[\frac{\bar{\pi}_A}{2} + \delta V_B^p\right] \tag{30}$$

$$+ \alpha_A(1 - \alpha_B)\left[\frac{\bar{\pi}_B}{2} + \delta V_A^p\right] + \alpha_A\alpha_B\left[\delta V_{AB}^p\right]$$

$$\geq (1 - \alpha_A)(1 - \alpha_B)\left[\frac{\bar{\pi}_A}{2} + \bar{\pi}_B + \delta V_B^p\right] + (1 - \alpha_A)\alpha_B\left[\frac{\bar{\pi}_A}{2} + \delta V_B^p\right]$$

$$+ \alpha_A(1 - \alpha_B)\left[\bar{\pi}_B + \delta V_{AB}^p\right] + \alpha_A\alpha_B\left[\delta V_{AB}^p\right]$$

and

$$(1 - \alpha_A)(1 - \alpha_B)\left[\frac{\overline{\pi}_A + \overline{\pi}_B}{2} + \delta V^c\right] + (1 - \alpha_A)\alpha_B\left[\frac{\overline{\pi}_A}{2} + \delta V_B^p\right] \quad (31)$$

$$+\alpha_A(1 - \alpha_B)\left[\frac{\overline{\pi}_B}{2} + \delta V_A^p\right] + \alpha_A\alpha_B\left[\delta V_{AB}^p\right]$$

$$\geq \quad (1 - \alpha_A)(1 - \alpha_B)\left[\overline{\pi}_A + \overline{\pi}_B + \delta V_{AB}^p\right] + (1 - \alpha_A)\alpha_B\left[\overline{\pi}_A + \delta V_{AB}^p\right]$$

$$+\alpha_A(1 - \alpha_B)\left[\overline{\pi}_B + \delta V_{AB}^p\right] + \alpha_A\alpha_B\left[\delta V_{AB}^p\right]$$

$\overline{V}_J$ and (29)-(31) may be written more compactly as maximizing

$$\overline{V}_J = (1 - \alpha_A)\frac{\overline{\pi}_A}{2} + (1 - \alpha_B)\frac{\overline{\pi}_B}{2} + (1 - \alpha_A)(1 - \alpha_B)\delta V^c + (1 - \alpha_A)\alpha_B\delta V_B^p + \quad (32)$$

$$\alpha_A(1 - \alpha_B)\delta V_A^p + \alpha_A\alpha_B\delta V_{AB}^p$$

subject to

$$(1 - \alpha_B)\delta[V^c - V_A^p] + \alpha_B\delta[V_B^p - V_{AB}^p] \geq \frac{\overline{\pi}_A}{2} \quad (33)$$

$$(1 - \alpha_A)\delta[V^c - V_B^p] + \alpha_A\delta[V_A^p - V_{AB}^p] \geq \frac{\overline{\pi}_B}{2} \quad (34)$$

$$(1 - \alpha_A)(1 - \alpha_B)\delta[V^c - V_{AB}^p] + (1 - \alpha_A)\alpha_B\delta[V_B^p - V_{AB}^p] + \alpha_A(1 - \alpha_B)\delta[V_A^p - V_{AB}^p] \quad (35)$$

$$\geq \quad (1 - \alpha_A)\frac{\overline{\pi}_A}{2} + (1 - \alpha_B)\frac{\overline{\pi}_B}{2}$$

These constraints simply state that the expected loss from a given defection must outweigh the expected gain from that defection. Consider (33), for example. Defecting in market A only changes payoffs if A is in the high demand state. If so, then a player gains $\frac{\overline{\pi}_A}{2}$ by defecting. If market B is in the high demand state, then play moves from σ^c to σ_A^p, inducing loss $(V^c - V_A^p)$ one period in the future. If market B is in the low demand state, then play moves from σ_B^p to σ_{AB}^p, inducing loss $(V_B^p - V_{AB}^p)$ one period in the future. If the expected loss exceeds the expected gain, then defection will not occur. The same analysis applies to (34) and (35).

Lemma 1 *In equilibrium, at least one of (33) and (34) must bind.*

Proof of Lemma 1: Suppose (33) and (34) both are slack. If (33) is slack, then $V_A^p = V^c$. This is the case because increasing V_A^p increases the objective function and relaxes both (34) and (35). Similarly, if (34) is slack, then $V_B^p = V^c$. Substitute the new values of V_A^p and V_B^p into (33)-(35), then add (33) and (34) after premultiplying them by $(1 - \alpha_A)$ and $(1 - \alpha_B)$, respectively. This summation yields

$$(1 - \alpha_A)\alpha_B\delta[V^c - V_{AB}^p] + \alpha_A(1 - \alpha_B)\delta[V^c - V_{AB}^p] > (1 - \alpha_A)\frac{\overline{\pi}_A}{2} + (1 - \alpha_B)\frac{\overline{\pi}_B}{2},$$

whereas (35) is

$$(1 - \alpha_A)(1 - \alpha_B)\delta[V^c - V_{AB}^p] + (1 - \alpha_A)\alpha_B\delta[V^c - V_{AB}^p] + \alpha_A(1 - \alpha_B)\delta[V^c - V_{AB}^p]$$
$$\geq (1 - \alpha_A)\frac{\overline{\pi}_A}{2} + (1 - \alpha_B)\frac{\overline{\pi}_B}{2}.$$

Consequently, if (33) and (34) both are slack, then (35) also must be slack. In equilibrium, all three incentive constraints cannot be slack.

Lemma 2 *Suppose (33) and (33) both bind. Then the solution that maximizes $\overline{V}_J$ and that satisfies (33)-(35) is*

$$\overline{V}_J = \frac{(1 - 2\alpha_A)\overline{\pi}_A}{2(1 - \delta)} + \frac{(1 - 2\alpha_B)\overline{\pi}_B}{2(1 - \delta)},$$

with

$$V_A^p = \frac{[2(1 - \alpha_A)\delta - 1]\overline{\pi}_A}{2\delta(1 - \delta)} + \frac{(1 - 2\alpha_B)\overline{\pi}_B}{2(1 - \delta)},$$

$$V_B^p = \frac{(1 - 2\alpha_A)\overline{\pi}_A}{2(1 - \delta)} + \frac{[2(1 - \alpha_B)\delta - 1]\overline{\pi}_B}{2\delta(1 - \delta)},$$

and

$$V_{AB}^p = \frac{[2(1 - \alpha_A)\delta - 1]\overline{\pi}_A}{2\delta(1 - \delta)} + \frac{[2(1 - \alpha_B)\delta - 1]\overline{\pi}_B}{2\delta(1 - \delta)},$$

subject to the feasibility constraints.

Proof of Lemma 2: Multiply (33) by $(1 - \alpha_A)$ and (34) by α_B. Substitute $(1 - \alpha_A)\alpha_B\delta V_B^p$ from (33) into $\overline{V}_J$, (34), and (35). The sign of the coefficient on V_A^p in (34) is ambiguous, so substitute V_{AB}^p from (34) into $\overline{V}_J$ and (35). Increase V^c in (35) until (35) just binds. This yields $\delta V_A^p = \delta V^c - \frac{\overline{\pi}_A}{2}$, so substitute V_A^p from (35) into $\overline{V}_J$. Using $V^c = \overline{V}_J$ yields

$$\overline{V}_J = \frac{(1 - 2\alpha_A)\overline{\pi}_A}{2(1 - \delta)} + \frac{(1 - 2\alpha_B)\overline{\pi}_B}{2(1 - \delta)}.$$

Moving backward through the proof yields the values for V_A^p, V_B^p, and V_{AB}^p.

Lemma 3 *Suppose (33) binds and (34) is slack. Then the solution that maximizes $\overline{V}_J$ and that* *satisfies (33)-(35) is*

$$\overline{V}_J = \frac{(1 - 2\alpha_A)\overline{\pi}_A}{2(1-\delta)} + \frac{(1-\alpha_B)\overline{\pi}_B}{2(1-\delta)},$$

with

$$V_B^p = \overline{V}_J,$$

subject to

$$V_A^p > \frac{[2(1-\alpha_A)\delta - 1]\overline{\pi}_A}{2\delta(1-\delta)} + \frac{\overline{\pi}_B}{2(1-\delta)} - \frac{\alpha_B[(1+\alpha_A)\delta - 1]\overline{\pi}_B}{2\alpha_A\delta(1-\delta)},$$

$$V_{AB}^p < \frac{[2(1-\alpha_A)\delta - 1]\overline{\pi}_A}{2\delta(1-\delta)} + \frac{(1-\alpha_B)[(1+\alpha_A)\delta - 1]\overline{\pi}_B}{2\alpha_A\delta(1-\delta)},$$

and the remaining feasibility constraints. The case of (33) being slack and (34) binding is analyzed in symmetric fashion, with a change of subscripts.

Proof of Lemma 3: First note that if (33) binds and (34) is slack, then $V_B^p = V^c$. Therefore, (35) holds strictly and is superfluous. Eliminate V_A^p using (33). Multiply (33) by α_A and (34) by $(1 - \alpha_B)$. Substitute $\alpha_A(1-\alpha_B)\delta V_A^p$ from (33) into $\overline{V}_J$ and (34). From these manipulations one determines that

$$\overline{V}_J = \frac{(1 - 2\alpha_A)\overline{\pi}_A}{2(1-\delta)} + \frac{(1-\alpha_B)\overline{\pi}_B}{2(1-\delta)}$$

and

$$V_{AB}^p < \frac{[2(1-\alpha_A)\delta - 1]\overline{\pi}_A}{2\delta(1-\delta)} + \frac{(1-\alpha_B)[(1+\alpha_A)\delta - 1]\overline{\pi}_B}{2\alpha_A\delta(1-\delta)}.$$

Now work backwards to determine V_A^p. From (33),

$$V_A^p > \frac{[2(1-\alpha_A)\delta - 1]\overline{\pi}_A}{2\delta(1-\delta)} + \frac{\overline{\pi}_B}{2(1-\delta)} - \frac{\alpha_B[(1+\alpha_A)\delta - 1]\overline{\pi}_B}{2\alpha_A\delta(1-\delta)}.$$

One also must ensure that V_A^p and V_{AB}^p satisfy the feasibility constraints. For $V_A^p \leq \overline{V}_J$, it must be the case that

$$\frac{[2(1-\alpha_A)\delta - 1]\overline{\pi}_A}{2\delta(1-\delta)} + \frac{\overline{\pi}_B}{2(1-\delta)} - \frac{\alpha_B[(1+\alpha_A)\delta - 1]\overline{\pi}_B}{2\alpha_A\delta(1-\delta)} < \frac{(1 - 2\alpha_A)\overline{\pi}_A}{2(1-\delta)} + \frac{(1-\alpha_B)\overline{\pi}_B}{2(1-\delta)}.$$

This is equivalent to

$$\alpha_B\overline{\pi}_B < \alpha_A\overline{\pi}_A.$$

If the preceding relationship holds, then there exists V_A^p satisfying the incentive and feasibility constraints.

For $V_{AB}^p \geq 0$, it must be the case that

$$0 < \frac{[2(1-\alpha_A)\delta - 1]\overline{\pi}_A}{2\delta(1-\delta)} + \frac{(1-\alpha_B)[(1+\alpha_A)\delta - 1]\overline{\pi}_B}{2\alpha_A\delta(1-\delta)}.$$

There are four cases to consider.

1) If $[2(1-\alpha_A)\delta - 1] \geq 0$ and $[(1+\alpha_A)\delta - 1] \geq 0$, then the preceding relationship holds easily and there exists V_{AB}^p satisfying the incentive and feasibility constraints.

2) If $[2(1-\alpha_A)\delta - 1] < 0$ and $[(1+\alpha_A)\delta - 1] < 0$, then the preceding relationship holds only for $\overline{\pi}_A = \overline{\pi}_B = 0$.

3) If $[2(1-\alpha_A)\delta - 1] \geq 0$ and $[(1+\alpha_A)\delta - 1] < 0$, then the preceding relationship holds only if

$$\overline{\pi}_B < \frac{\alpha_A[2(1-\alpha_A)\delta - 1]\overline{\pi}_A}{(1-\alpha_B)[1-(1+\alpha_A)\delta]}.$$

4) If $[2(1-\alpha_A)\delta - 1] < 0$ and $[(1+\alpha_A)\delta - 1] \geq 0$, then the preceding relationship holds only if

$$\overline{\pi}_A < \frac{(1-\alpha_B)[(1+\alpha_A)\delta - 1]\overline{\pi}_B}{\alpha_A[1-2(1-\alpha_A)\delta]}.$$

Proof of Proposition 5: Suppose that some collusion can be sustained in each market in the non-coordinated equilibrium. That is, $2(1-\alpha_A)\delta - 1 \geq 0$ and $2(1-\alpha_B)\delta - 1 \geq 0$. If α_A, α_B, and δ are such that $(1+\alpha_A)\delta - 1 < 0$ and $(1+\alpha_B)\delta - 1 < 0$, then Case 3 of Lemma 3 applies. As a first step, suppose that (33) binds and (34) is slack. For the solution in Lemma 3 to apply, it must be the case that

$$\alpha_B\overline{\pi}_B < \alpha_A\overline{\pi}_A$$

and

$$\overline{\pi}_B < \frac{\alpha_A[2(1-\alpha_A)\delta - 1]\overline{\pi}_A}{(1-\alpha_B)[1-(1+\alpha_A)\delta]}.$$

Setting $\overline{\pi}_A = \pi^m$ relaxes the preceding constraints. Because $\alpha_B \leq \alpha_A$, the first constraint holds for all feasible $\overline{\pi}_B$. If α_A is sufficiently small, then the second constraint requires $\overline{\pi}_B < \pi^m$. In fact, for α_A sufficiently small, the second constraint will just bind. Hence, I can write

$$\overline{V}_J = \frac{(1-2\alpha_A)\pi^m}{2(1-\delta)} + \frac{(1-\alpha_B)}{2(1-\delta)}\left[\frac{\alpha_A[2(1-\alpha_A)\delta - 1]\overline{\pi}_A}{(1-\alpha_B)[1-(1+\alpha_A)\delta]}\right],$$

which simplifies to

$$\overline{V}_J = \frac{(1 - 3\alpha_A)\pi^m}{2\left[1 - (1 + \alpha_A)\,\delta\right]}.$$

For α_A and α_B sufficiently small, the preceding value for $\overline{V}_J$ is strictly less than the profits obtained in the non-coordinated equilibrium, in which each market is treated separately.

A symmetric argument holds if (33) is slack and (34) binds.

Proof of Proposition 6: Suppose that no collusion can be sustained in either market in the non-coordinated equilibrium. That is, $2\left(1 - \alpha_A\right)\delta - 1 < 0$ and $2\left(1 - \alpha_B\right)\delta - 1 < 0$.

First, if α_A, α_B, and δ are such that $(1 + \alpha_A)\,\delta - 1 < 0$ and $(1 + \alpha_B)\,\delta - 1 < 0$, then Case 2 of Lemma 3 applies. In this instance, no collusion can be sustained using multimarket contact. Hence, multimarket contact does not increase profit.

Second, if α_A, α_B, and δ are such that $(1 + \alpha_A)\,\delta - 1 \geq 0$ and $(1 + \alpha_B)\,\delta - 1 \geq 0$, then Case 4 of Lemma 3 applies. As a first step, suppose that (33) binds and (34) is slack. For the solution in Lemma 3 to apply, it must be the case that

$$\alpha_B \overline{\pi}_B < \alpha_A \overline{\pi}_A$$

and

$$\overline{\pi}_A < \frac{(1 - \alpha_B)\left[(1 + \alpha_A)\,\delta - 1\right]\overline{\pi}_B}{\alpha_A\left[1 - 2\left(1 - \alpha_A\right)\delta\right]}.$$

The preceding two constraints can be combined to yield a new constraint,

$$\alpha_B \overline{\pi}_B < \frac{(1 - \alpha_B)\left[(1 + \alpha_A)\,\delta - 1\right]\overline{\pi}_B}{\left[1 - 2\left(1 - \alpha_A\right)\delta\right]},$$

that also must be satisfied for the solution in Lemma 3 to apply. This combined constraint may be simplified to

$$0 < \left[(1 + \alpha_A)\left(1 - \alpha_B\right) + 2\left(1 - \alpha_A\right)\alpha_B\right]\delta - 1.$$

For α_A and α_B sufficiently large, this constraint cannot hold. In this instance, no collusion can be sustained using multimarket contact. A symmetric argument holds if (33) is slack and (34) binds. Hence, α_A and α_B sufficiently large, multimarket contact does not increase profit.

Proof of Proposition 7: Suppose that α_A and δ are such that $2\left(1 - \alpha_A\right)\delta - 1 < 0$ and $(1 + \alpha_A)\,\delta - 1 \geq 0$. In this instance it must be the case that $\alpha_A \geq \frac{1}{3}$. Further, suppose that $\alpha_B \leq \frac{2}{3}$. In this instance, Case 4 of Lemma 3 applies. As a first step, suppose that (33) binds and (34) is slack. For

26

the solution in Lemma 3 to apply, it must be the case that

$$\alpha_B \bar{\pi}_B < \alpha_A \bar{\pi}_A$$

and

$$\bar{\pi}_A < \frac{(1 - \alpha_B)\left[(1 + \alpha_A)\delta - 1\right]\bar{\pi}_B}{\alpha_A\left[1 - 2(1 - \alpha_A)\delta\right]}.$$

Combining the preceding two constraints, and recalling that $\alpha_A \geq \frac{1}{3}$, it must be the case that

$$\alpha_B < \frac{(1 + \alpha_A)\delta - 1}{(3\alpha_A - 1)\delta}.$$

That is, α_B must be sufficiently small for multimarket contact to increase profits. For example, if $\alpha_A = 0.4$ and $\delta = 0.75$, then α_B must be less than $\frac{1}{3}$. Suppose $\alpha_B = 0.1$. Then the constraints all can be satisfied with $\bar{\pi}_A = \bar{\pi}_B = \pi^m$, and the resulting payoffs are

$$\bar{V}_J = 2.2\pi^m \quad V_A^p = 1.8\pi^m \quad V_B^p = 2.2\pi^m \quad V_{AB}^p = 0.033\pi^m$$

The maximal profit when employing multimarket contact exceeds the maximal profit in the non-coordinated equilibrium, which is $1.6\pi^m$.

Proof of Proposition 8: First, suppose that some collusion can be sustained in each market in the non-coordinated equilibrium. That is, $2(1 - \alpha_A)\delta - 1 \geq 0$ and $2(1 - \alpha_B)\delta - 1 \geq 0$. If α_A, α_B, and δ are such that $(1 + \alpha_A)\delta - 1 \geq 0$ and $(1 + \alpha_B)\delta - 1 \geq 0$, then Case 1 of Lemma 3 applies. In this instance, multimarket contact increases profits.

Second, suppose that no collusion can be sustained in either market in the non-coordinated equilibrium. That is, $2(1 - \alpha_A)\delta - 1 < 0$ and $2(1 - \alpha_B)\delta - 1 < 0$. If α_A, α_B, and δ are such that $(1 + \alpha_A)\delta - 1 \geq 0$ and $(1 + \alpha_B)\delta - 1 \geq 0$, then Case 4 of Lemma 3 applies. As a first step, suppose that (33) binds and (34) is slack. For the solution in Lemma 3 to apply, it must be the case that

$$\alpha_B \bar{\pi}_B < \alpha_A \bar{\pi}_A$$

and

$$\bar{\pi}_A < \frac{(1 - \alpha_B)\left[(1 + \alpha_A)\delta - 1\right]\bar{\pi}_B}{\alpha_A\left[1 - 2(1 - \alpha_A)\delta\right]}.$$

Combining the preceding two constraints, it must be the case that

$$\alpha_B < \frac{(1 - \alpha_B)\left[(1 + \alpha_A)\,\delta - 1\right]}{\left[1 - 2\,(1 - \alpha_A)\,\delta\right]}.$$

This combined constraint may be simplified to

$$0 < \left[(1 + \alpha_A)(1 - \alpha_B) + 2\,(1 - \alpha_A)\,\alpha_B\right]\delta - 1.$$

This constraint holds if both α_A and α_B are close to $\frac{1}{2}$, for δ sufficiently large. For example, if $\alpha_A = \alpha_B = \frac{1}{2}$, then δ must exceed $\frac{4}{5}$. As both α_A and α_B get sufficiently large, then the combined constraint cannot hold. Therefore, for moderate degrees of uncertainty, multimarket contact increases profits even though no collusion could be sustained in the non-coordinated equilibrium.

References

[1] Abreu, D., Pearce, D., and Stacchetti, E. "Optimal Cartel Equilibria with Imperfect Monitoring." *Journal of Economic Theory,* Vol. 39 (1986), pp. 251-269.

[2] Abreu, D., Pearce, D., and Stacchetti, E. "Toward a Theory of Discounted Repeated Games with Imperfect Monitoring." *Econometrica,* Vol. 58, No. 5 (1990), pp. 1041-1063.

[3] Barla, P. "Multimarket Contact and Pricing Strategy in the U.S. Domestic Airline Industry." Cornell University Ph.D. Dissertation (1994).

[4] Bernheim, B. Douglas and Whinston, Michael D. "Multimarket Contact and Collusive Behavior." *RAND Journal of Economics,* Vol. 21, No. 1 (1990), pp. 1-26.

[5] Evans, W. and Kessides, I. "Living by the 'Golden Rule': Multimarket Contact in the U.S. Airline Industry." *Quarterly Journal of Economics,* Vol. 109, No. 2 (1994), pp. 341-366.

[6] Feinberg, R. and Sherman, R. "An Experimental Investigation of Mutual Forbearance by Conglomerate Firms," in *Industry Structure and Performance,* Schwalbach, J. (ed.). Berlin: Bohn, Sigma (1985), pp. 139-166.

[7] Feinberg, R. and Sherman, R. "Mutual Forbearance Under Experimental Conditions." *Southern Economic Journal,* Vol. 54, No. 4 (1988), pp. 985-993.

[8] Gertner, R. and McCutcheon, B. "Multimarket Contact and Tacit Collusion with Imperfect Monitoring." mimeo (1994).

[9] Green, E., and Porter, R. "Noncooperative Collusion Under Imperfect Price Information." *Econometrica,* Vol. 52 (1984), pp. 87-100.

[10] Parker, P. and Roller, L. "Collusive Conduct in Duopolies: Multimarket Contact and Cross-Ownership in the Mobile Telephone Industry." CEPR Discussion Paper 989 (1994).

[11] Phillips, O. and Mason, C. "Mutual Forbearance in Experimental Conglomerate Markets." *RAND Journal of Economics*, Vol. 23, No. 3 (1992), pp. 395-414.

[12] Singal, V. "Airline Mergers and Multimarket Contact." *Managerial and Decision Economics*, Vol. 17, No. 6 (1996), pp. 559-574.

[13] Tirole, J. *The Theory of Industrial Organization.* Cambridge, Mass.: M.I.T. Press (1988).

Figure 1

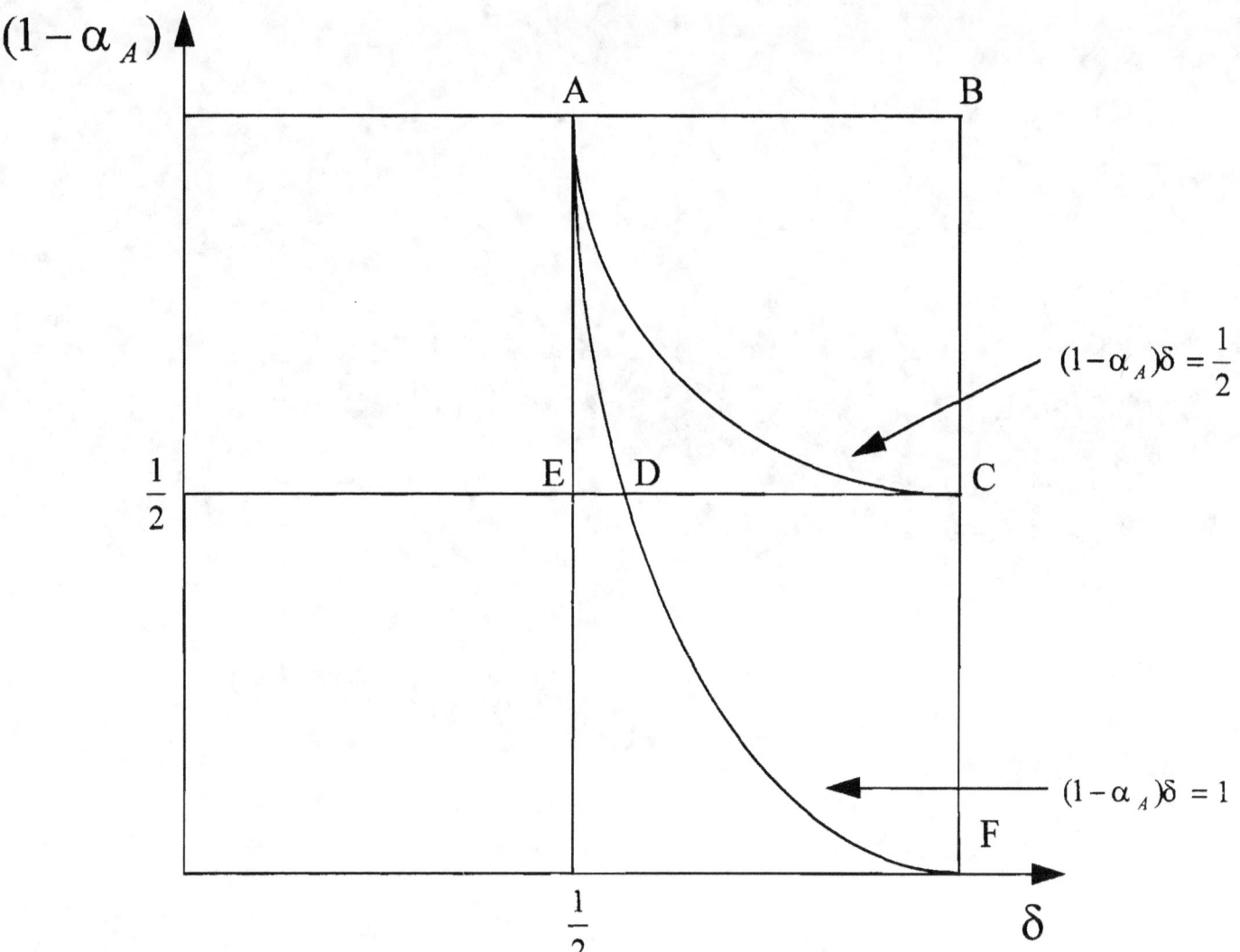

www.ingramcontent.com/pod-product-compliance
Lightning Source LLC
Chambersburg PA
CBHW081317180526
45170CB00007B/2740